Finn MacCool

and the Giant's Causeway

Written by John Dougherty

Illustrated by Lee Cosgrove

OXFORD
UNIVERSITY PRESS

Chapter 1

 Long, long ago, there lived in Ireland a mighty giant by the name of Finn MacCool. Finn was taller than an oak tree and stronger than a dozen oxen. He was brave and kind, but he was also very proud.

"I am the greatest giant of them all!" he would boast. "There is no one who can beat me!"

Across the sea in Scotland, there lived another giant. This one was called Angus. He was huge and strong, with an angry red face, and everyone feared him.

One day, Angus was told of Finn's boasting. When he heard that Finn thought he was the greatest giant of all, Angus flew into a rage.

"I am the greatest giant!" he roared. "I'll teach Finn a lesson he won't forget!"

Angus strode angrily to the shore. He looked across at Ireland. Cupping his hands to his mouth, he bellowed, "Hey! Finn MacCool! Come and see what a *real* giant looks like, you great baby!"

The breeze carried his words to Finn and when Finn heard them, his temper rose. Standing on the cliffs of County Antrim, he roared back, "All I see is a giant fool!"

At this, Angus shook with anger. "If I could only get across the sea to you ...!" he shouted. "I would teach you a lesson you'd never forget!"

"That's easily done!" Finn replied. He tore a great rock from the cliffs and hurled it into the waves – the first stone of a giant pathway across the sea.

Angus began to do the same, but as the giants drew closer to one another Finn began to worry. He was getting tired, and Angus did look very big, and very strong.

So Finn hurried home to his wife, Oona. She was not as big or as strong as he was, but she was very clever. He told her all about Angus, and the path across the sea.

Oona sighed. "Finn," she said, "you're being a big baby."

"I am not being a baby!" Finn said.

Oona put a baby's bonnet on his head. "You are now,"
she told him, and she gave him a nightgown and made their
bathtub look like a giant cot. "Lie down," she told Finn, "and
leave Angus to me."

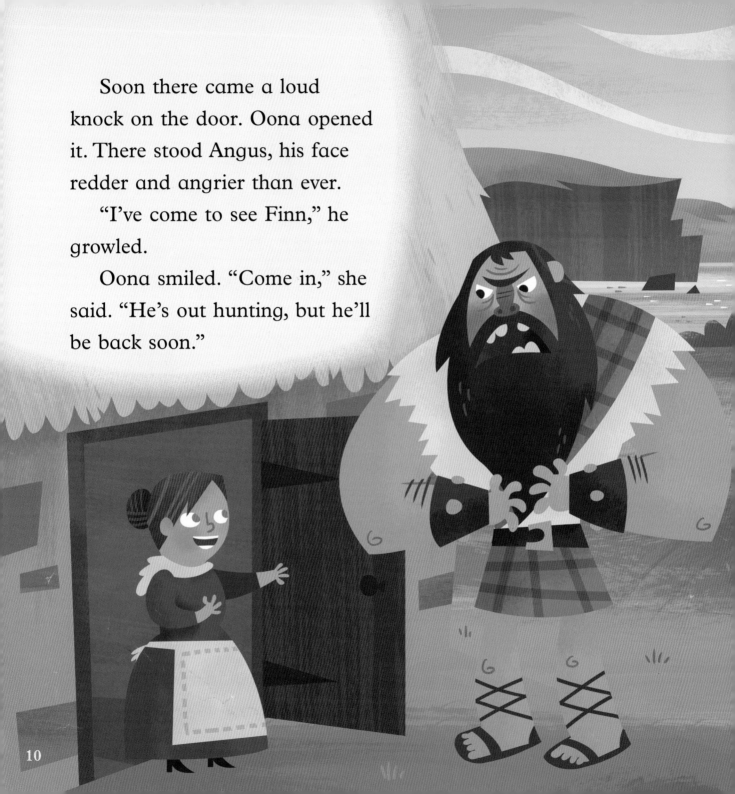

Soon there came a loud knock on the door. Oona opened it. There stood Angus, his face redder and angrier than ever.

"I've come to see Finn," he growled.

Oona smiled. "Come in," she said. "He's out hunting, but he'll be back soon."

Chapter 2

 "Are you a friend of Finn's?" Oona asked.

"No," snarled Angus. "I've come to show him that I'm stronger than he is."

"Really?" said Oona. "A little fellow like you?"

"Little?" said Angus crossly. "I'm the biggest giant there is!"

Oona smiled. "I don't mean to be rude," she said, "but you're hardly bigger than Finn's baby." And she nodded at the cot where Finn lay staring up with wide, nervous eyes.

"Goo, goo," said Finn.

Angus looked at the cot. "My!" he said. "What a big baby!"

"Not really," Oona said. "Not when you think how big his daddy is."

Now Angus began to worry. If Finn's baby was so big, Finn must be much bigger!

"Still," he said, "Finn may be big, but he can't be as strong as I am!"

In his cot, Finn felt the house move. He put his thumb in his mouth and sucked it, worrying. Angus must be very strong to do such a thing.

At last, Angus finished turning the house.
"There!" he said proudly.

"Well done," said Oona. "Finn can do it much faster than that, mind you."

Angus' face fell.

"But that wasn't bad for such a little fellow," Oona went on. "You must be tired now. Come in and have a snack."

Chapter 3

 Angus went in and sat down. Oona gave him a cake. She had just made it, and it was still hot.

"Try this," she said. "Finn likes nothing better than one of these cakes after he's been working hard."

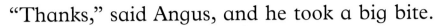
"Thanks," said Angus, and he took a big bite.

But Angus did not know that Oona had baked a stone inside the cake.

"Ow!!!" he yelled.

"What's wrong?" Oona asked.

"I broke my tooth on your cake!" Angus howled.

"Really?" said Oona. "You must have very soft teeth. Finn loves these cakes. So does the baby," she added. She gave a cake to Finn, but she was careful to give him a cake without a stone inside. Finn ate it in three big bites.

"More!" he said. "Mammy! More!"

Angus stared.

"That baby must have very strong teeth!" he said.

Oona smiled. "Not really," she said. "Not when you think how strong his daddy is. You can feel them if you like."

So Angus put his hand in
Finn's mouth, to feel his teeth ...

24

... and Finn bit as hard as he could. Angus yelled with pain.

Just then, Oona said, "I think I hear Finn coming home."

Angus' red face turned pale. If Finn's baby was so strong, Finn must be much stronger.

"Is that the time?" he said. "I'm sorry, but I have to go."

"Angus fight Daddy!" said Finn.

"Not today," Angus said.

"Angus fight baby!" said Finn, and he jumped out of the cot.

This was too much for Angus. He turned and ran. "Help!" he cried. "There's a giant baby after me!"

He ran all the way back to Scotland, tearing up the path so that neither Finn nor the giant baby could follow.

And Finn and his clever wife laughed and laughed, knowing that Angus would never again cross the sea to Ireland in search of the mighty Finn MacCool.

If you ever go to County Antrim, you may see the few rocks that Angus left behind. They are still called the Giant's Causeway, and they are one of the wonders of the world.

Once upon a time...

The end.